# TALES OF DEVOTION

## A Bridge for Lord Rama

A Bridge for Lord Rama
Published by Isvara Dasa
Text copyright © 1994 by Mary Scioscia
Illustrations copyright © 1994 by Loetitia S. Lilot

Second Edition 2019

ISBN: 978-81-940279-9-7

Our Other Children Books Series:
Better English with Krishna
Bhrgu's Test
Dog and the Wolf and other Stories from Pancatantra
Hari's Adventure in Port-of-Spain
Adventures from India (Blue Prince and Golden Prince Series)
Gita Stories from Padma Purana
Great Heroes of Mahabharat Series
The Ten Incarnations Coloring Book
Kanaya's Bull
Sweet Pastimes of Damodara Coloring Book
My First Lord Jagannatha Book

If you are interested in the purchasing or the distribution of this book
or any of the above publications, you may contact:

Touchstone Media

Shri Krishna Sharnam, Block B #206

Vrindavan, Mathura Dist., 281121, UP INDIA

www.touchstonemedia.com

E-mail : sales@touchstonemedia.com

All rights reserved. Printed in India. No part of this book may be used or
reproduced in any manner whatsoever without written permission except in the
case of brief quotations embodied in critical articles or reviews.

# A BRIDGE FOR LORD RAMA

Published by Isvara Dasa

Retold by Mary Scioscia

Illustrations and lettering by
Loetitia S. Lilot (Saradiya dasi)

TOUCHSTONE
MEDIA
*Matter for the Soul*

Lord Rama set out to rescue her. To get to Ravana's home, he had to cross the part of the ocean that lies between India and Sri Lanka.

Lord Rama called for the monkey, Nila to build a bridge for him. Millions of monkeys came to help Nila. Some uprooted giant trees. Others dragged them to the shore and heaved them into the water.

Hanuman, the son of the windgod, led a group of other monkeys who lifted huge rocks the size of mountains. They pushed and pulled and shoved them into the ocean.

Squirrel watched Hanuman and Nila and the other monkeys. He thought, "I love Lord Rama. I want to help build this bridge for him too." He couldn't pull up a big tree by its roots. He couldn't push huge rocks. He looked at the pebbles and small stones at the water's edge. He looked at his short legs.

"I know what I'll do!" said Squirrel. And he picked up countless pebbles and small stones and dropped them into the ocean to help build up the pile of logs and rocks.

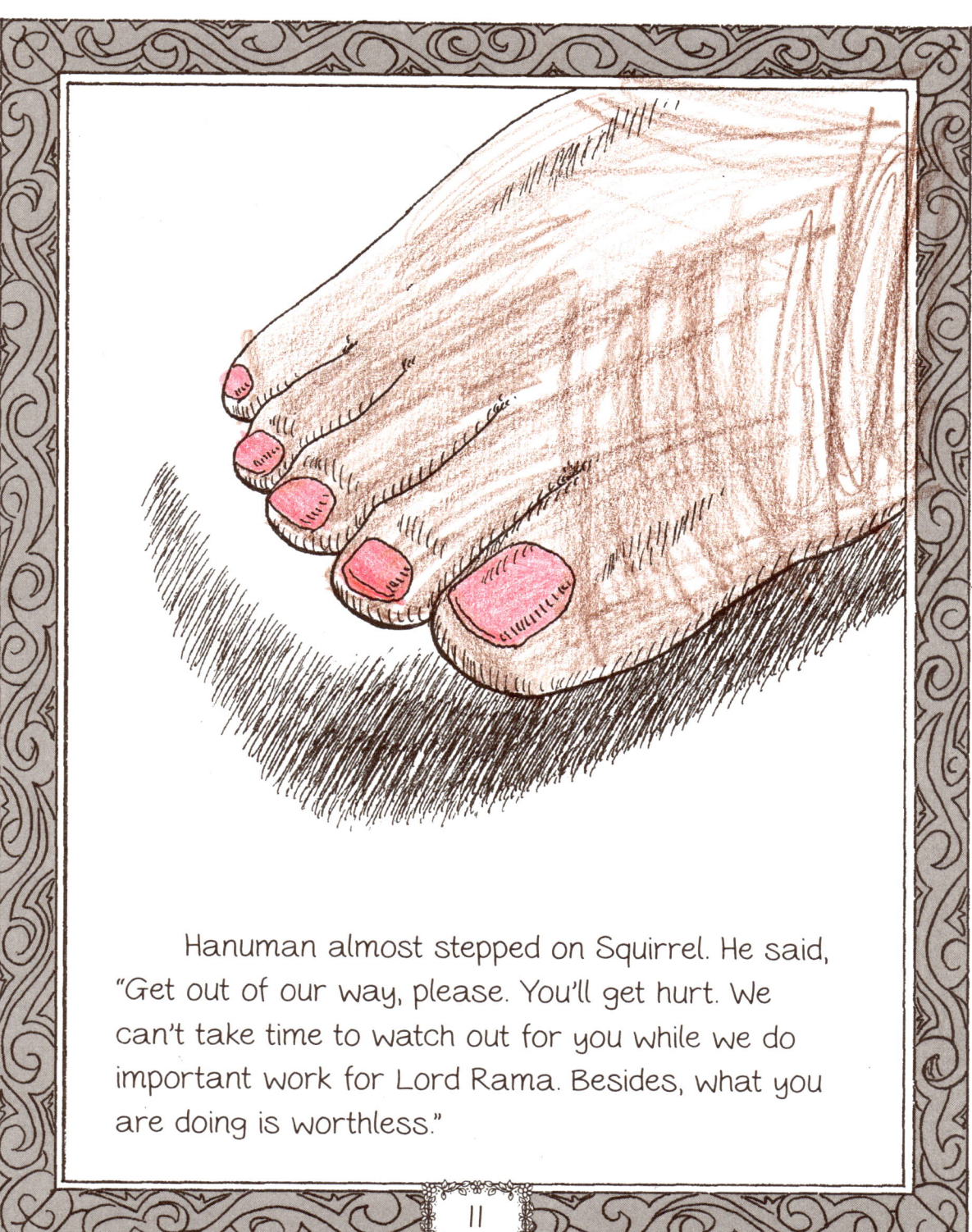

Hanuman almost stepped on Squirrel. He said, "Get out of our way, please. You'll get hurt. We can't take time to watch out for you while we do important work for Lord Rama. Besides, what you are doing is worthless."

Lord Rama heard Hanuman and instantly appeared before him. "Do not speak disrespectfully to Squirrel," the Lord said. "Do not belittle his labor. You and he each do the most you can. "And you each do it with love and devotion. To me your service is equal."

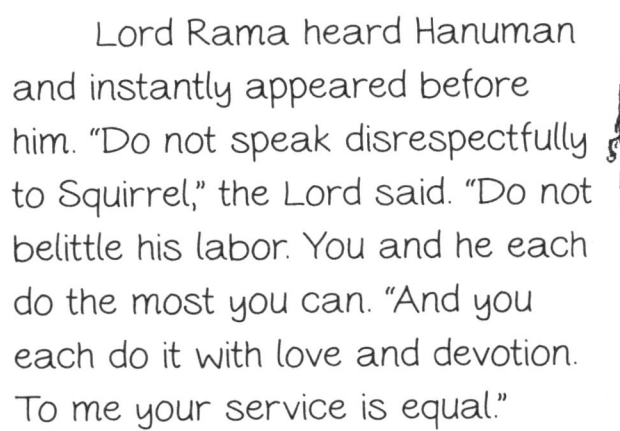

When he heard this, Hanuman understood that if he truly loved the Lord, he must treat Squirrel and his work with respect.

On the fifth day they completed the last segment of the bridge. It went right up to Mount Suvela on Sri Lanka. The monkeys formed a line to parade across the bridge.

Just behind them, Lord Rama rode on the back of Hanuman.

"Hanuman, may I sit there, too?" Squirrel asked. Hanuman reached out and set Squirrel on his shoulder where he could see everything.

There were so many monkeys, they couldn't all squeeze onto the bridge. Some dived into the water and swam across. Others spread their wings and flew.

From the sky, the demigods showered bright colored, sweet smelling flowers onto the crowd below. They sang out to Lord Rama, "Oh Supreme Lord: Rescue your wife, Conquer your enemies, Rule over the seas for numberless years."

# CHILDREN'S COLLECTION

**BETTER ENGLISH WITH KRISHNA**
ABC Coloring Book

**GITA STORIES**
From the Padma Purana
Colored Version

**GITA STORIES**
From the Padma Purana
Black & White Version

**THE TEN INCARNATIONS**
Coloring Book

**BHRGU'S TEST**
Bhrgu Muni's quest on Who is the Supreme

**ADVENTURES FROM INDIA**
Blue Prince Volume 1

**ADVENTURES FROM INDIA**
Blue Prince Volume 2

**ADVENTURES FROM INDIA**
Blue Prince Volume 3

**ADVENTURES FROM INDIA**
Blue Prince Volume 4

**SWEET PASTIMES OF DAMODARA**
Coloring Book

**GREAT HEROES OF MAHABHARATA**

Arjuna

**GREAT HEROES OF MAHABHARATA**

Karna

**GREAT HEROES OF MAHABHARATA**

Bhisma

**GREAT HEROES OF MAHABHARATA**

Vidura

**GREAT HEROES OF MAHABHARATA**

Kunti & Draupadi

**KANAYA'S BULL**
And other Stories

**GOLDEN PRINCE VOL 1**

**GOLDEN PRINCE VOL 2**

**DOG AND THE WOLF**
Stories from Pancatantra
Coloring Book

**HARI'S ADVENTURE IN PORT OF SPAIN**

**KRISHNA SHOWS FOR CHILDREN**
4 DVD set

**SONGS FOR KRISHNA'S KID**
Learning Shastra
Audio CD

**MY FIRST LORD JAGANNATHA BOOK**
Jagannathas illustrated story Book

All our products are available for bulk or single purchases.
Phone: +91 8336916108,
E-mail: sales@touchstonemedia.com

www.touchstonemedia.com